The Sun

by David M. Haugen

KidHaven Press, an imprint of Gale Group, Inc.
10911 Technology Place, San Diego, CA 92127

Library of Congress Cataloging-in-Publication Data
Haugen, David M.
   The sun/by David M. Haugen.
      p. cm.—(Eyes on the sky)
   Includes bibliographical references.
   Summary: Discusses the sun and its function in our solar system, including its visible features and the importance of the sun's energy.
   ISBN 0-7377-0674-0 (lib. : alk. paper)
   1. Sun—Juvenile literature. [1. Sun.] I. Title. II. Eyes on the Sky (San Diego, Calif.)
   QB521.5 .H38 2002
   523.7—dc21

   00-012815

Cover Photo: NASA, Mark Marten/Photo Researchers, Inc.
© Paul Almasy/CORBIS, 15
Alex Bartel/Science Photo Library/Photo Researchers, Inc., 38
© Bettmann/CORBIS, 17
© Sheldon Collins/CORBIS, 31
Division of Tourism, 35
© R.W. Jones/CORBIS, 5
NASA, 20, 22, 27, 39
NASA, Mark Marten/Photo Researchers, Inc., 29
© Gianni Dagli Orti/CORBIS, 13
Photodisc, 11
George Post/Science Photo Library/Photo Researchers, Inc., 26
Martha Schierholz and Chris Jouan, 6, 8, 10, 14, 16, 19, 21, 33, 36

Copyright 2002 by KidHaven Press, an imprint of Gale Group, Inc., 10911 Technology Place, San Diego, CA 92127

No part of this book may be reproduced or used in any other form or by any other means, electrical, mechanical, or otherwise, including, but not limited to, photocopying, recording, or any information storage and retrieval system, without prior written permission from the publisher.

Table of Contents

Chapter 1
A Medium-Sized Star 4

Chapter 2
The Solar System 12

Chapter 3
A Giant Nuclear Furnace 18

Chapter 4
Visible Features of the Sun 25

Chapter 5
The Importance of the Sun's Energy 32

Glossary 41
For Further Exploration 44
Index 46
About the Author 48

1 A Medium-Sized Star

The sun is a star. Like other stars in the universe, the sun is made up of burning gases that glow and give off light that can be seen on Earth. The sun is about 93 million (93,000,000) miles from Earth. This may seem like a very long distance, but it is short compared with the next closest star, Proxima Centauri, that is about 25 trillion (25,000,000,000,000) miles away.

The sun looks so much bigger than other stars because of its nearness to Earth. When compared to other stars, however, it is average in size. Astronomers refer to the sun as a medium-sized star because some stars are larger and others are smaller. Compared with the Earth and the other planets in the solar system, the sun is gigantic. The sun's diameter (the distance from one side to the other, traveling straight through the middle) is

864,400 miles. Earth's diameter is only about 8,000 miles. If hollowed out, the sun could hold 1.3 million Earths. Not even Jupiter, the largest planet in the solar system, is close in size to the sun.

The sun is approximately 93 million miles from the Earth.

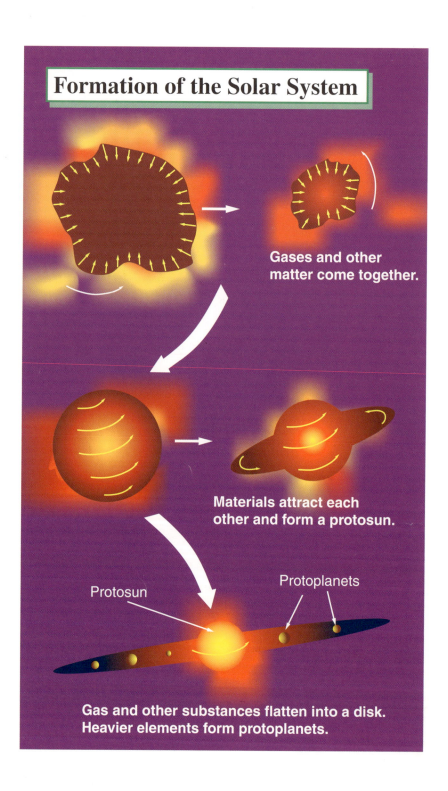

Forming the Sun

The huge sun that shines so brightly today was formed nearly 5 billion years ago. At that time, large amounts of dust and gases (mostly hydrogen) came swirling together by chance. The gases and other matter formed a young star, or protosun. As the **protosun** took shape in the center of the vast whirlpool of gas, the remaining gas and other substances flattened into a huge disk billions of miles wide. Within the huge disk, smaller whirlpools of gas, called protoplanets, formed. These would later become Earth, Mercury, Venus, and the other planets.

The Planets Are Formed

Over time, the dust and gases of the protosun became more and more tightly packed. A dense, ball-like shape emerged and began to heat up. When the temperature was very high, a chain reaction, or series of explosions, occurred, and the sun began to shine.

Heat and energy from the first explosions allowed the sun's rays to push away the remaining gas of the whirling disk, leaving only the heavier protoplanets behind. The nine planets of the solar system stayed close to their present locations, circling the fiery sun. Scientists believe it took about 80 million years for the sun to reach its present size and heat output. During that time the planets continued to form. While that was happening, the rest of the early gas cloud had been pushed away by the sun's energy, and the solar system began looking much like it does today.

The Sun's Future

The sun's light and heat have been bathing the Earth in much the same way ever since it reached its current size. This is because the

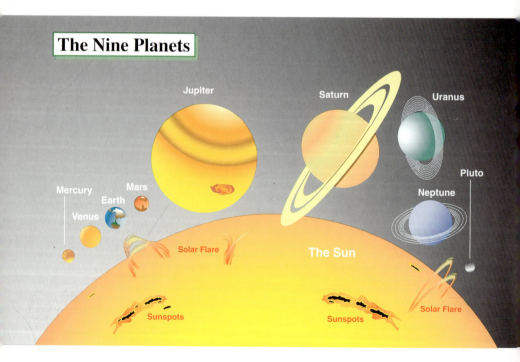

sun has been using up hydrogen gas—its fuel source—at a fairly constant rate since becoming a medium-sized star billions of years ago. The sun uses 600 to 700 million tons of hydrogen every second. This gives an idea of how much of the gas the sun holds. Since it formed, the sun has used up only about half its supply of hydrogen. Scientists think there is still enough hydrogen in the sun to burn for 6.4 billion years.

When that time arrives, astronomers believe the sun will grow in size. Although no one knows for sure what will happen, the sun is expected to turn into a mammoth star called a **red giant**, able to produce even greater amounts of light and heat. The nearest planets will suffer as their surfaces are scorched by the heat. The oceans and other waterways on Earth will boil away. All life on the planet will come to an end.

The Death of the Sun

The sun's future is less certain. Some astronomers think that the sun will cool and shrink after a couple of million years at this expanded size. They base this belief on what they see happening to stars that are dying now. These dying stars are called **white dwarfs**. Scientists think that white dwarfs continue to emit light for billions of years as they slowly decay and collapse in on themselves. If these theories are correct, when the sun burns out completely, it will become just another floating mass in space, smaller than the Earth.

Other scientists, however, believe that the sun will keep expanding once it has become a red giant. According to this theory, the sun will grow bigger and bigger until it explodes in a giant flash of light called a nova. All the sun's planets would be destroyed in such an

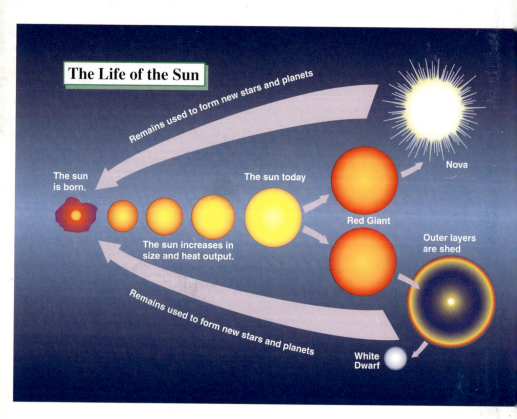

The sun will continue to burn for many billions of years to come.

explosion. From the ashes of the nova, a new star might form, and maybe new planets would follow, repeating the story of the birth of the solar system. Whichever theory comes true, the sun has billions of years left to shine as it does now.

2
The Solar System

The solar system contains the sun and the planets that rotate around it. All the planets circle the sun in paths called **orbits**. The sun holds the planets in their orbits through **gravity**, a force of attraction. On Earth, gravity pulls objects toward the ground. In a similar way, the sun's gravity tries to draw the planets toward it. The planets never "fall" into the sun because the sun's gravity is not strong enough to overcome the other forces that keep the planets moving through space. If the sun's gravity disappeared, the planets would shoot off into space. But as long as the sun's gravity attracts them, the planets will continue to circle the sun.

A Sun-Centered Solar System

In ancient times, astronomers mistakenly believed that the sun and all the planets were

Ptolemy believed the sun and the planets orbited the Earth.

orbiting the Earth. This idea resulted from seeing the sun rise in the east and set in the west every day. It seemed that the Earth stood still while the sun traced an arc through the sky over and over. Around A.D. 150, a Greek scientist named Ptolemy gave support to this idea when he created a model of the universe. In his model, the sun orbited the unmoving Earth. Ptolemy's model was widely accepted for hundreds of years.

Then, in the late 1400s, about thirteen hundred years after Ptolemy proposed his

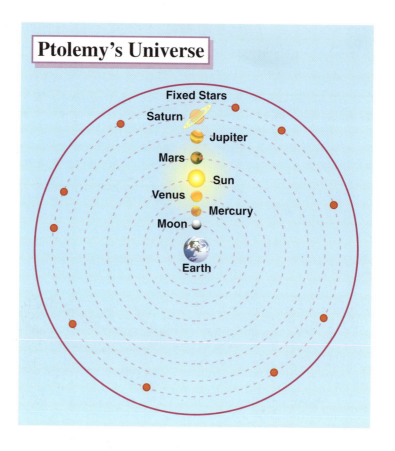

model, a Polish scientist named Nicolaus Copernicus proposed a new idea. Copernicus believed the sun, and not the Earth, is at the center of the heavens and that the planets revolve around the sun. Copernicus's ideas did not gain acceptance among other scientists until 1543, but even then his theory proved not completely correct. For one thing, Copernicus believed that the planets orbited the sun in perfect circular motion. He lacked the tools to see that this was not true. In 1609, a German astronomer, Johannes Kepler, concluded that the sun is indeed at the center of the solar system, just as Copernicus had said. However, Kepler suggested that the planets trace somewhat flattened circular orbits around the sun rather than truly round paths. This model was more realistic than Copernicus's. It also showed that the Earth is nearer to the sun in some parts of the year

Polish scientist Nicolaus Copernicus proposed that the planets revolved around the sun.

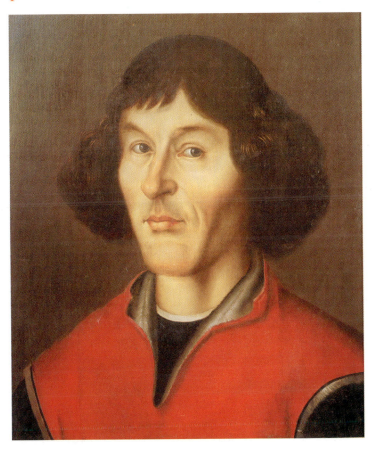

than it is in others. For instance, in July the Earth is about 3 million miles further from the sun than it is in January. This is because in January the planet travels along a flatter portion of its orbit, whereas in July it travels along the sharply curved part.

Kepler's changes improved the accuracy of the sun-centered model of the solar system, as

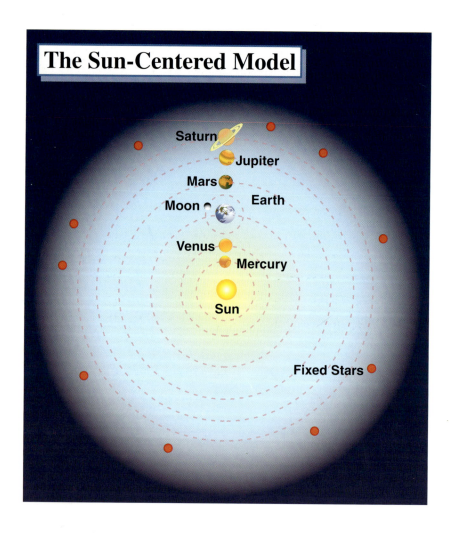

German astronomer Johannes Kepler suggested the planets orbited the sun in a flattened circular path.

did later changes. But the basic Copernican idea—so revolutionary in its time—became accepted as fact. With the laws of planetary motion settled, astronomers and other scientists could turn their attention to the make-up of the planets and even the sun itself.

3
A Giant Nuclear Furnace

A huge, fiery body like the sun produces a great deal of energy. Just as a campfire burns wood to make energy in the form of heat and light, the sun burns fuel to produce its energy. The fuel that feeds the sun's fire is a very common element in the universe: hydrogen gas. On Earth, hydrogen is most commonly found in water, where it is locked together with oxygen. In the sun, hydrogen is a free element, but it undergoes a change as it is used up by the sun.

Since the sun has so much gas and dust squeezed together in a confined space, there is a lot of pressure within the fiery mass. In fact, the pressure increases dramatically toward the center of the sun. Here, at the very heart of the sun, hydrogen gas is under so much pressure that its atoms break up. The

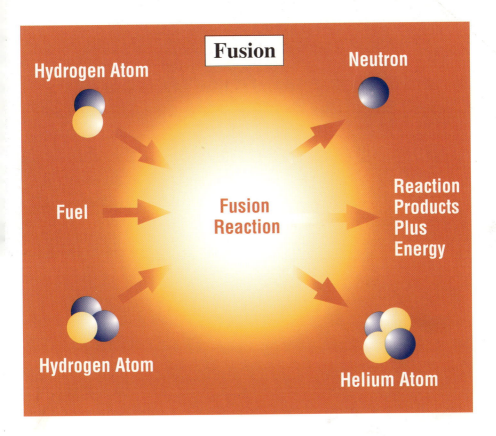

process changes some of the hydrogen into a heavier gas called helium, while the rest of the hydrogen is released as pure energy. The change from hydrogen to helium is called nuclear fusion, and it occurs in all stars.

The sun uses millions of tons of hydrogen in nuclear fusion reaction, which will continue until all its hydrogen is used up. As the sun's hydrogen runs out, the forces of nuclear fusion will begin to convert the helium. When this gas, too, has run out, the sun will begin the process of expanding into a red giant star.

Energy from Deep Within

The nuclear reactions that cause fusion of the sun's gases start in the center of the sun, or the core. Scientists think that the sun's **core** is 100,000 miles in diameter, about the size of the planet Jupiter. The temperature in the core is very high. On Earth, water boils at 212 degrees Fahrenheit, and even iron will melt if heated to 5432 degrees Fahrenheit. But to keep the nuclear fusion reactions going, the sun's core

The sun's core can reach 28 million degrees Fahrenheit.

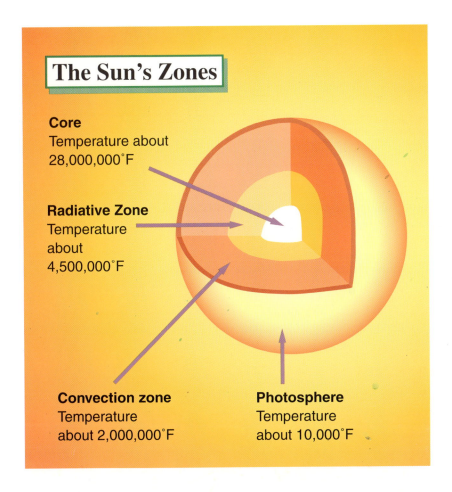

The Sun's Zones

Core
Temperature about 28,000,000°F

Radiative Zone
Temperature about 4,500,000°F

Convection zone
Temperature about 2,000,000°F

Photosphere
Temperature about 10,000°F

must reach temperatures as high as 28 million (28,000,000) degrees Fahrenheit. This solar energy produced in the reactions pushes upward through the other layers of the sun.

Astronomers cannot see inside the sun but they assume that the energy produced in the core is changed during the push through the upper layers. This theory makes sense because the outer layers of the sun are cooler than the center. The types of nuclear reaction

A Giant Nuclear Furnace 21

taking place in the very hot inside are different from the types that occur at the lower temperatures of the outer layers.

The Energy Path

Scientists believe that the energy from the sun's core is transmitted in the form of waves as it passes through the gases in the layer

Energy from the sun's core is transmitted as waves.

that surrounds the core. These energy waves next reach a cooler zone, just below the visible surface of the sun.

Scientists believe that as the temperatures change, the wave energy may be turned into a superheated current of gas. They suspect that this is because photographs of the sun's surface show areas of tightly packed dark and light areas, like piles of black and white rice grains. They assume that this pattern results from jets of superheated gases shooting up toward the sun's surface.

When the energy reaches the top layer of the sun, the reactions occur at temperatures around 10,000 degrees Fahrenheit, instead of millions of degrees as in the sun's core. Once out of the top layer, the energy passes through the sun's atmosphere and spreads into space. Earth and the other planets receive this energy in the form of heat, light, and other forms of **radiation**.

Gravity Within the Sun

If the sun could not release its energy, it would explode. But how does the sun keep from coming apart as energy pushes toward the surface? One might think that all the violent reactions would simply cause the sun to break apart, scattering its gases as the energy bubbled up from the core. But this never happens. The sun is held together by gravity, the same gravity that pulled gases and dust together as the sun was forming billions of years ago. The gravity that holds the sun together also balances the force of the energy that escapes it. So, the sun not only remains intact, it stays about the same size. Not all stars, however, maintain this balance, and some either grow or shrink over time. Although the sun is not alone in having a balance of forces, the balance ensures that Earth and the other planets receive the light and heat energy they need.

Guesswork and Observation

Despite all that astronomers believe to be true about the inner workings of the sun, they do not know for sure whether their theories are correct. Because no one can see into the sun—and no space probe could survive its heat—scientists base their theories on how similar reactions occur in nuclear power plants or nuclear research laboratories on Earth. However, astronomers also know a great deal about the sun as a result of what they have observed with the help of special telescopes. So many things happen on the visible surface of the sun that scientists learn more about this fascinating star every day.

4
Visible Features of the Sun

Studying the sun by looking at it directly is not possible. The sun is so bright on most days that it can be difficult to observe closely and may temporarily blind anyone staring at it. Even during a total solar eclipse, when the sun is less bright, it cannot be viewed directly without risk of eye damage.

In a total solar eclipse, the moon moves between the earth and the sun, blocking the sun's rays. Total solar eclipses occur yearly, but the most spectacular effect—a narrow ring of fiery, pinkish light visible along the sun's edge in a dark sky—cannot be seen everywhere on Earth in every eclipse.

The Chromosphere and the Corona

The ring of light that can be seen during an eclipse is called the **chromosphere**. The chromosphere is the sun's inner atmosphere. Just as the Earth has an atmosphere of nitrogen, oxygen, and carbon dioxide, the sun has an atmosphere of hydrogen and helium gas. The chromosphere is about 9,000 miles thick, and in its upper reaches, the temperature can be as high as 40,000 degrees Fahrenheit.

Surrounding the chromosphere is the jagged edge of the sun, the outer atmosphere or **corona**. Also visible during an eclipse, the corona extends millions of miles into space,

The sun's rays are blocked by the moon in a solar eclipse.

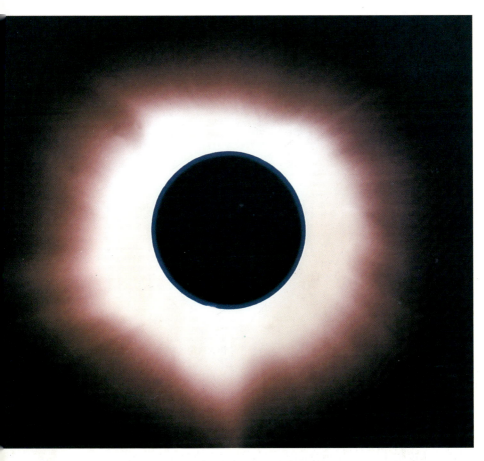

A ring of light called the chromosphere can be seen during an eclipse.

and the part nearest the sun appears as a thicker white crown of light. The gases here can reach temperatures in the millions of degrees Fahrenheit, much hotter than the gases in the chromosphere. Astronomers can view the corona with special instruments called **coronagraphs** that photograph the white crown while blocking out the blinding main

Visible Features of the Sun

body of the sun. The coronagraph allows astronomers to study the corona daily, rather than waiting for a solar eclipse.

Solar Activity

One of the most interesting types of solar activity that people on Earth can see—at the time of an eclipse or with the aid of a coronagraph is a **solar prominence**. Solar prominences are giant loops of flaming gas that project outward from the rim of the chromosphere. Most are tens of thousands of miles high, but some have reached as far as a million miles into space. A solar prominence can appear and disappear in a matter of hours, or it may be visible for days.

Another type of fiery activity on the sun causes **solar flares**. Solar flares are not as large as prominences and they do not last as long either. A solar flare looks like a brighter patch of light against the sun's already bright outer layer. Like a signal flare on Earth, a solar flare brightens for a short time and then dims. Astronomers say that these flares, lasting from a few minutes to several hours, can arc up to 10,000 miles into the sun's atmosphere.

Solar flares and prominences send great amounts of heat, light, and radiation into space. The radiation from the powerful solar flares reaches Earth partly in the form of highly charged particles called ions, which can disrupt electrical systems of homes and businesses. Television and radio signals can become hazy or scrambled, and magnetic compasses may spin off course.

Sunspots

Astronomers link both solar prominences and solar flares to storms on the sun's surface.

Sunspots appear as dark places on the sun's surface.

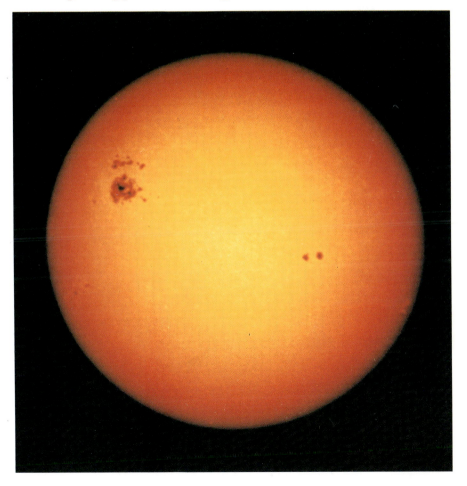

Visible Features of the Sun

Such storms, called **sunspots**, appear as vast, dark, swirling patches in photographs. Sunspots are not commonly seen in the sun's outer layer but solar flares erupt out of them, while solar prominences often arch near the area where sunspots tend to occur.

Sunspots appear dark to an observer because they are cooler than the gases around them. Scientists do not know what causes this temperature difference. Some assume that cooler gases from inside the sun break through the superheated gases of the outer atmosphere and temporarily create these dark regions. Others believe that the sunspots are caused by magnetic storms which keep some of the light and heat underneath from escaping.

The timing of the appearance of sunspots is also mysterious, although they are known to arise in a cycle that spans about eleven years. Small spots appear in the early years of the cycle, and with each year, more sunspots dot the sun. At the end of the cycle, many large sunspots arise that can sometimes be seen without the aid of a telescope. No one is sure why this pattern develops, but astronomers have found that it is predictable.

The regions of the sun in which sunspots appear correspond to the eleven-year cycle. Sunspots spread out along belts that lie between the middle—or equator—of the sun and the sun's north and south poles. At the

View of Manhattan at sunrise, seen from Weehawken, New Jersey.

beginning of a cycle, the small sunspots appear closer to the poles. By the end of the cycle, the large sunspots sit near the equator.

Odd Phenomena

The causes of sunspots, solar flares, and solar prominences remain a mystery. So far they do not seem to have an effect on the Earth. But the sun does influence life on Earth in many important ways.

5
The Importance of the Sun's Energy

Although scientists are unsure what part the sun played in the creation of life on Earth, they agree that light and heat from the sun were very important. Most scientists believe that carbon, oxygen, nitrogen, and hydrogen mixed on Earth approximately 4.5 trillion (4,500,000,000,000) years ago and, with the proper amount of heat and light from the sun, formed living organisms. The sun's steady, continual bathing of the Earth's surface gave these early life-forms the chance to develop into plants and animals.

Over billions of years of evolution, plants and animals—including human beings—reached the state they exist in today. And the sun continues to play a vital part in evolution. Most important, the sun keeps plant life alive and growing on Earth. Plant life is important because plants not only provide food for humans and animals but also produce much of the oxygen that living creatures breathe. Without the sun, the plants could not exist. All life would suffer and eventually die out for lack of food and oxygen.

Photosynthesis

Plants grow and produce oxygen through a process called **photosynthesis**. Photosynthesis starts when sunlight touches the leaves of a plant. The sun's energy breaks down water

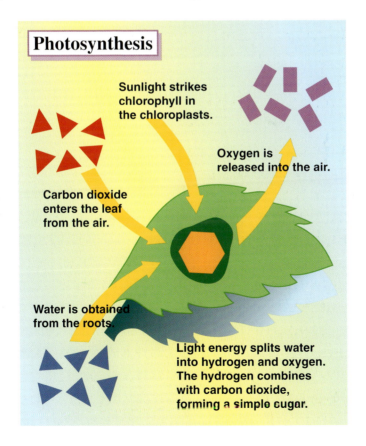

molecules held in the plant's leaves. This process releases oxygen into the air for people and animals to breathe. This process also releases hydrogen. The hydrogen mixes with some of the oxygen and with the carbon dioxide gas that plants also take in through their leaves. Carbon dioxide is the gas people and animals exhale. When it combines with oxygen and hydrogen, simple sugars form.

The simple sugars in the plants are as important as oxygen to continuing life on the planet. Animals and people benefit from consuming these sugars in two ways. Either they eat vegetables or other plants that contain these sugars, or they eat animals that have eaten these plants. The sun is directly responsible for making both simple sugars and oxygen. Without sunlight, photosynthesis could not take place.

Energy in the Earth

Living things store the sun's energy, and some of this supply remains even after plants and animals die. The energy that went into making sugars in a plant remains in those carbon compounds and returns to the soil when the plant decays. The same is true of animals and humans that have died and decomposed in the ground. Since life has been on the planet in one form or another for billions of years, a huge amount of energy is locked up in the

Photosynthesis begins when sunlight reaches plants.

earth. And every generation of life covers all or part of the layers of earth used by earlier generations. The weight of each new layer of earth adds pressure to these buried remnants of living matter, called fossils, crushing them and converting their long-stored energy into another form.

These energy forms, known as fossil fuels, exist deep under the earth. Their common

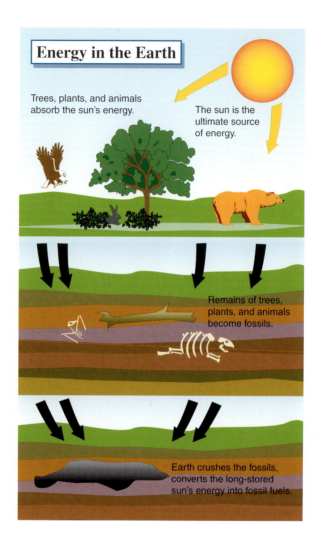

names are coal, oil, peat, lignite, and natural gas. When humans discovered fossil fuels, they burned them to release their energy as heat. People originally used the heat to cook food and warm themselves, but in the eighteenth century, inventors learned how to turn the heat energy into other forms of energy such as electricity and steam. These forms of energy provide light and help run machines today, making life easier for many people.

Solar Energy

In addition to fossil fuels, people have used the direct heat of the sun as a source of energy. They make use of the sun's power by capturing the heat of its rays. For example, sunlight was used long ago to clean water for drinking in a process called distillation. First the sun's heat was used to turn water into steam, leaving the heavier impurities behind. Then the steam was turned back into water by cooling it. The resulting water was clean and drinkable. Distillation processes today often use fossil fuels to boil the water because they are not limited to daytime use. Many inventors, however, are experimenting with new ways to cheaply and effectively distill large amounts of water with pure sunlight.

   Scientists still have much to learn about ways of using solar energy. They have not yet figured out how to harness the energy of the sun efficiently. To run most machines, solar energy needs to be converted into electrical energy. Solar cells that would do this work quickly and easily have yet to be invented. Most **solar cells** today are not efficient. They take great amounts of sunlight but produce only a weak electric current. Therefore it is still cheaper to obtain energy by burning fossil fuels.

Solar Energy in the Home

Although solar energy devices still need a lot of improvement, they are growing in popularity. One reason for this is that they do not pollute like fossil fuels do. Some houses have solar panels on the roof to collect sunlight and turn it into electrical energy to power lights and some home appliances. Solar water heaters are

Solar panels turn sunlight into electrical energy.

Many satellites use solar panels for energy.

now used in some homes to burn gas, and to provide hot water for sinks, showers, and bathtubs. These devices do not work well enough yet to provide all the power a home may need. But solar energy can replace at least part of the fossil fuels needed to run a household. This may do away with some of the pollution caused by burning fossil fuels. Some day in the future if solar cells are perfected there might be no need for burning fossil fuels at all.

Looking Toward the Future

Although solar energy has yet to satisfy human energy needs in the United States, it has become an important part of the nation's space program. This is because it is cheaper to use solar energy than fossil fuels to move spacecraft that have left Earth's atmosphere. A fossil fuel source onboard a spacecraft would require a lot of storage room and would add a great deal of weight to the ship. Solar panels are relatively light and can be counted on to work as long as they are exposed to the sun. Presently, many satellites and space probes carry solar panels to catch the sun's rays and power the instruments on board. If human beings someday hope to travel to other planets, they will have to learn more about putting solar energy to use. Both solar energy and the sun itself will continue to be important in the future of humankind.

Glossary

chromosphere: The sun's inner atmosphere.

core: The innermost part of the sun. The nuclear reactions which produce the sun's energy start at the core.

corona: The visible outer atmosphere of the sun. It appears as the jagged crown of light that surrounds the sun.

coronagraph: An astronomical instrument that allows scientists to study the sun's corona by blocking the bright center of the sun from the observers' view.

gravity: The force of attraction. Gravity on Earth draws all matter toward the ground. Gravity in the sun holds the gases in the ball shape visible in the sky.

orbit: The path of one heavenly body revolving around another. The revolving body is held in orbit partly by the gravity of the central body. This helps explain why an orbiting body continues to revolve around the central body instead of flying off into space.

photosynthesis: The process by which green plants turn carbon dioxide into oxygen.

protosun: The protosun was the earliest form of the sun as its components came together from the giant swirling mass of gases and solid elements that developed into the solar system.

radiation: Generic name for any energy that comes from nuclear reactions. The sun's energy is a form of radiation that reaches Earth as light and heat.

red giant star: A huge star that produces great quantities of light and heat. Some stars turn into red giants as they get older and start to run out of fuel. Some astronomers believe the sun will eventually turn into a red giant.

solar cell: A device that converts solar energy into electrical energy.

solar flare: A burst of light from the sun's photosphere that can last for minutes or hours.

solar prominence: Larger and longer lasting than solar flares, solar prominences are huge arcs of light that shoot out from the sun's photosphere. Like solar flares, they are made up of hot jets of burning gas.

sunspots: Mysterious dark patches that appear in an eleven-year cycle along the face of the sun. Their dark appearance is thought to be due to temperatures cooler than the surrounding photosphere.

white dwarf star: A dying star that is collapsing in on itself. Red giant stars that have used up all their hydrogen and helium turn into white dwarf stars.

For Further Exploration

Paulette Bourgeois, *The Sun*. Buffalo, NY: Kids Can Press, 1997. This book, in the *Starting with Space Series*, provides basic yet interesting information on the sun. It also couples the information with illustrative experiments that readers can try at home.

Robert Daily, *The Sun*. New York: Franklin Watts, 1994. A simple, informative book about the sun. It is easy to read and has a glossary of terms.

Michael Daley, *Amazing Sun Fun Activities*. New York: Learning Triangle Press, 1998. This is an excellent book that helps readers learn facts about the sun through simple experiments that can be conducted at home.

William Jaber, *Exploring the Sun*. New York: Julian Messner, 1980. A good resource that is easy to read and follow. It includes black-and-white photos and illustrations and a helpful glossary.

David C. Knight, *The First Book of the Sun*. New York: Franklin Watts, 1968. Although more than thirty years old, this book is still a great resource. It has many good black-and-white photos. It also provides an informative chapter on the role of the sun in many early religions.

Index

animals, 32–34

carbon dioxide, 26, 32, 34
chromosphere, 25–27
coal, 36
Copernicus, Nicolaus, 14–15, 17
corona, 26, 27
coronagraphs, 27–28

Earth, 7, 18, 20, 25
  atmosphere of, 26
  end of life on, 9
  energy stored in, 34–36
  influence of sun on, 31–33
  light and heat for, supplied by sun, 24
  position in solar system, 14
    early beliefs about, 13
    variation of, over course of year, 15–16
  size of, compared to sun, 4–5
  solar activity visible from, 28–29

electricity, 36–37
energy, 7, 18, 33
  in Earth, 34–36
  in sun's core, 22–23
  see also solar energy
equator, 31

fossil fuels, 35–38, 40
  need for, 39

gravity, 12, 24

heat, 9, 23, 24, 36
  from explosions during formation of sun, 7
  output of, from sun, 8, 32
  variations of, in sun, 29
  see also solar energy
helium, 19, 26
hydrogen, 9, 18–19, 32, 34

Jupiter, 20

Kepler, Johannes, 14–16

light, 10
  in photosynthesis, 33–34

of sun, 8, 11, 32
   brightness of, 25
   see also chromosphere;
     solar flare
lignite, 36

Mercury, 7
moon, 25

nitrogen, 26, 32
nova, 10–11
nuclear fusion, 19–24

oil, 36
oxygen, 18, 26, 32–34

peat, 36
photosynthesis, 33–34
planets, 32
   effects of sun's gravity
     on, 12
     place in solar system
       and, 13–15
   formation of, 7–8
   orbits of, 12
   see also solar system
plants, 32–34
pollution, 39
protoplanets, 7
protosun, 7
Proxima Centauri, 4
Ptolemy, 13–14

radiation, 23, 28
red giant, 10, 19

satellites, 40
solar cells, 37
solar eclipse, 25–28
solar energy, 37–40
   part of U.S. space program, 40

solar flare, 28–30
solar prominence, 28–30, 31
solar system, 7, 8, 11
   ancient ideas about, 12–13
   Copernican ideas about, 14, 17
   Kepler's model of, 15–16
stars, 4–5, 7, 24
   formation of, 11
   known as white dwarfs
     when dying, 9–10
sun, 8
   brightness of, 25
   core of, 20–21
   different theories about, 10–11
   distance of, from Earth, 4
   energy produced by, 18
     transmitted from core, 22–23
   formation of, 7
   future of, 9, 19
   gravity of, 12, 24
   inner atmosphere of, 26
   place of, in solar system, 13–17
   role of, in life on Earth, 32–35
   size of, 5
   see also solar energy;
     solar flare; sunspots
sunspots, 29–31

Venus, 7

water, 9, 18, 20
   steam energy and, 36, 37
white dwarfs, 9–10

About the Author

Author David M. Haugen edits books for Lucent Books and Greenhaven Press. He holds a master's degree in English literature and has also worked as a writer and instructor.